HOW TO
AGGRAVATE
A <u>MAN</u>
EVERY TIME...

HOW TO AGGRAVATE A <u>MAN</u> EVERY TIME...

and have him beg for mercy!

BY CHRISTINA ARNESON
AND TERESA MCMILLIAN

ADAMS MEDIA CORPORATION
Holbrook, Massachusetts

Published by
Adams Media Corporation
260 Center Street, Holbrook, MA 02343

ISBN: 1-58062-214-3

Printed in the Canada.
J I H G F E D C B A

Library of Congress Cataloging-in-Publication Data
Arneson, Christina.
How to aggravate a man every time : and have
him beg for mercy / Christina Arneson.
p.   cm.
ISBN 1-58062-214-3
1. Man-woman relationships—Humor.
2. Men Humor. I. Title.
PN6231.M45A76   1999
818'.5402—dc21   99-15774
                        CIP

This book is available at quantity discounts for bulk purchases.
For information, call 1-800-872-5627.

Visit our home page at http://www.adamsmedia.com

CONTENTS

AN INSPIRATIONAL MESSAGE FROM THE AUTHORS

We're so proud to make this book available to all of the women who need it — and that's all of you!

This little book has been designed expressly to bring you hours of enjoyment. Read it and let that beautiful brain of yours go to work. Get your girlfriends involved. Start a movement. Come up with contests. Rate your successes with a numbering system of "aggravation factors." Use multiple aggravations as often as you can. Call your friends and brag about the last one you bagged. Just do it — get out there and aggravate the hell out of them!

And remember, you don't have to limit yourself to your husband or boyfriend. Aggravate the average Joe on the street! Aggravate the cable guy! Aggravate your brother and your male coworkers! Be really aggravating when a male telemarketer calls (ask him lots of questions)! Aggravate politicians and policy makers! Aggravate large companies! Aim high! Annoy every last one of them!

You can do it! We know you can! Now get out there, ladies, and start aggravating!

IF A MAN SPEAKS
IN THE FOREST
AND NO WOMAN IS
THERE TO HEAR

IS HE STILL WRONG?

Make the Most of PMS

♥ Be a drama queen.

♥ Cry for no reason at all.

♥ Practice to perfection a really great blank stare.

♥ Go to extreme measures to get attention.

♥ Learn to cry on demand.

♥ Every once in a while, just look annoyed and walk away—but don't explain why.

❤ Act really possessive of him.

❤ Act like you couldn't care less.

❤ Laugh to yourself every now and again—and when he asks you what you were thinking, say "Nothing."

❤ Cry over AT&T commercials.

❤ Bring up your tortured childhood as often as possible.

❤ Learn how to smile like the Mona Lisa.

♥ Start an argument every time something remotely negative happens in your life that has nothing to do with him. (If he presses the issue, you will be forced to make it his fault.)

♥ When fighting, alternate walking out and slamming the door with getting in his face and staying there.

♥ Say something to him and then deny it later. If he forces the issue, start crying.

♥ Make sure to explain all kinds of unrelated things in a conversation.

❥ Open the door crying if he comes home after two.

❥ Switch topics in the middle of a conversation and expect him to follow.

❥ Whine until you get your way, and then complain that you never get your way.

❥ Talk endlessly about a problem and get mad when he offers a solution.

❥ Tell him "I don't understand why you act this way." When he says "What way?" just cry and don't answer.

Aggravating the New Man in Your Life

But Harry my LAST boyfriend did that!

So go back out with HIM!

❣ Take over the remote control.

❣ Don't return his phone calls for two weeks, and then act like nothing is wrong.

❣ Tell him you "learned it on *Oprah*."

❣ When he asks you what you want to do that evening, tell him "Let's just talk."

❣ Remind him of your month-by-month anniversaries.

❣ Every single time you are within arm's reach, cop a feel. (*Warning:* Aggravation only occurs if you do it every single time!)

♥ Go simply ga-ga over little babies.

♥ Mention your biological clock.

♥ Counter his every opinion with that of your best friend.

♥ Tell him you just want to be "one of the guys."

♥ Wear lots of lipstick and gloss on dates.

♥ Ask him what his sign is, and then make him read the horoscope with you to see if you are compatible.

❤ Open doors for him on a date.

❤ Ask him to go with you for a psychic reading.

❤ Try to solve all of his problems for him. When he says he doesn't have any, tell him he's in denial.

❤ Make a really big deal about the holidays.

❤ Continually tell him he's different from any other boyfriend you've ever had, but don't explain how.

❤ If he tells you that he loves you, pat his cheek and say "That's nice."

❣ Write him long love letters and complain when he only responds with flowers.

❣ Refer to manly things as cute.

❣ Take as long as you can to get your point across.

❣ Pretend you know what you are talking about . . . especially when you don't.

❣ Be a cat person.

❣ Spend large portions of time talking about yourself, and then complain that you don't know anything about him.

❤ Talk about the guy your mother wanted you to marry.

❤ Make grand generalizations about men to his face.

❤ If he's alone, ask him what he's doing. When he says "nothing," tell him it's impossible to be doing nothing.

❤ When he's in a bad mood, keep asking him what's wrong.

❤ When he doesn't respond, call all of your girlfriends and tell them that he's in a bad mood but won't say what's wrong.

Aggravating His Friends with Yours

> Did I ever tell you guys about the time Tom cried when his hamster died

> Jeez Tom I never new you were so sensitive!

> Tell us the story TOM!

> Tom you never told us that story.

♥ Pretend you know what you are talking about when his friends are around.

♥ Tell a story in front of his best guy friends about something really "cute" he did.

♥ Tell a story in front of his guy buddies about something really intimate that he did.

♥ Set up your girlfriends with all of his friends, and make sure he knows it's his fault when their relationships don't work out.

♥ Smoke when you're out with your girlfriends . . . then give him a big, fat, breathy kiss when you get home.

💔 Have friends that you're not interested in having him meet.

💔 Ask him to lunch to meet your friends—lots of them—and then talk to your girlfriends so much that he can't get a word in edgewise.

💔 Call your friends immediately after every fight and tell them all the details.

💔 Call all your friends after every fight and tell them all the details, but make yourself sound like an angel and him like a big ogre.

💔 Flirt with his friends—but only after a fight.

♥ Invite your girlfriends over for a card game and . . .

spend more time talking than playing.

allow "do-overs."

change the rules in midplay to make it more fair for those who are losing.

at the end of the game, split up the money so everyone goes home with what they came with.

Then ask them back for the next weekend.

♥ Look better when you go out with your friends than when you go out with him.

♥ When you go out with your friends, stay out really late.

♥ Tell his friends about the time the two of you seriously discussed Viagra™.

♥ When his friends phone, talk to them for long periods of time about relationship matters.

♥ Find friends that will do the things that he won't.

♥ Ask his friends if he told them about your last big fight and who they thought was right.

♥ Wait up for him when he goes out with his friends.

Public Displays
of Aggravation

Ooooooo . . .
nice buns!

Geez, Wanda! Can't you wait
'til we get out of the church
before you start that!

♥ When he takes you out, complain that your feet hurt and you need a quick massage—then dance all night with anyone you can find.

♥ Touch him frequently in public.

♥ Pat him on the butt when he's trying to be respectable.

♥ When in public, point to a good-looking guy and ask your partner if he thinks the guy's "hot."

♥ Give him incomplete instructions on meeting him at a place he's never been. Then get mad when he's late.

❤ Sign up for six weeks of "couples cooking" classes.

❤ Invite him frequently to do things that you know he doesn't want to do.

❤ Make him take ballroom dancing lessons with you.

❤ And the whole time you're dancing tell him you're on air while you step on his feet.

❤ Plan dates really far in advance, don't remind him, and then get mad when he forgets about them.

♥ When you go out with him, start yawning at 9:30.

♥ Talk to him in public about natural bodily functions.

♥ Take several hours to get ready for a date, and then come out looking just like you did before you started.

♥ Accept an invitation for the two of you to attend an event you know he'll hate—without telling him.

♥ Or, tell him about it beforehand, and when he says no, buy nonrefundable tickets.

♥ Be overly loving in public . . . and really distant at home.

♥ When flying together, insist on the window seat and get up to stretch or to go to the bathroom every fifteen minutes.

♥ Order for him in a restaurant.

♥ Eat the food off his plate without asking.

♥ Order more food than you can eat in a week, and then push your plate away after a few bites.

❤ Eat very slowly when you know he wants to smoke a cigarette.

❤ Don't even make a move to pay the bill.

❤ Take a long time deciding what to eat in a restaurant. (If you have a male waiter, this is a double whammy.)

❤ Do the same at the bar (another double whammy).

❤ Talk to everyone you come into contact with, including waiters, bartenders, hostesses, busboys, ticket-takers, people in the car next to you, the man at the gas station . . .

Do I Look Fat to You?

♥ Show too much cleavage and get mad when he looks at it.

♥ Show no cleavage at all.

♥ Ask his advice on what you should wear, and then wear the opposite.

♥ Borrow his clothes and don't return them.

♥ Borrow his clothes and return them smelling like perfume.

♥ Buy him an abdominizer and show him how to use it.

♥ Notice a gray hair on his head and tell him you want to pull it.

♥ Give him a bottle of Grecian Formula™.

♥ Clean out his closet when he's not home and give the excess to charity.

♥ Cut your long hair—very short. Cry when he looks surprised.

♥ Invite him over for dinner and serve Healthy Choice™ frozen dinners.

♥ Go on a diet and expect him to eat what you eat.

❣ Make comments about his diet while
he's eating.

❣ Ask if he's going to finish that, pointing to
his plate after you ordered only a salad.

❣ Order more food than you can eat in a
week, and then say you are on a diet.

❣ Keep telling him you need to lose weight
until you sound like a broken record.

❣ Then go fix yourself a bowl of ice cream
with hot fudge and whipped cream.

♥ If he gives you a look, start crying and say he thinks you're fat.

♥ Run into the bedroom and slam the door. (Use the moment when he's throwing his hands up in the air and talking to God to grab your bowl of ice cream and bring it with you.)

♥ Come out later talking about this great show you were watching on TV.

6

Make Him Carry Your Purse

Grocery List for Steve

- ✓ milk
- ✓ bread
- ✓ ice cream
- ✓ cookies
- tampons
- maxi pads
- ✓ potato chips
- ✓ toilet paper
- ✓ laundry detergent

♥ Take him shopping with you, and make him hold your purse while you're in the dressing room or walking around the store to give you more freedom.

♥ Make him buy tampons for you.

♥ Send him to the store the same day you did the "big shopping."

♥ Buy him something you really intend to keep for yourself.

♥ Insist that you NEED to go shopping, and then don't buy anything.

♥ Send him to the store with coupons. Check the receipt to make sure he used them.

♥ Take him to Victoria's Secret and buy a flannel robe.

♥ Buy lots of little bottles of things to stuff the bathroom with and never use them. Position them to fall out of the medicine cabinet every time he opens it.

♥ Buy him new underwear that is too small.

♥ Buy him new underwear that is too big.

❤ Buy the clothes YOU want him to wear.

❤ Return the things he buys for you.

❤ Buy lots of things to take back later. Keep all your receipts, just in case.

The Joy of (Aggravating Men with) Sex

I really thought we could wait a bit longer

But Jane we've waited 5 years, and we're married!

❤ Don't jump in the sack right away. Assure him it's worth waiting for.

❤ Jump in the sack right away, and then complain how easy he was.

❤ Jump in the sack right away, and talk about how jumping in the sack right away has ruined all your past relationships (but that this one will be different!).

❤ Fake an orgasm with exaggerated detail. Then repeat the performance on the couch in your jammies while eating ice cream from the container with a big wooden spoon.

❤ Call him by your ex-boyfriend's name in bed.

❤ Giggle during sex.

❤ After sex, thank him instead of telling him you love him.

❤ After sex, make him stay awake and talk about your relationship.

❤ Push his head down (to indicate you'd like oral sex).

❤ Fall asleep during oral sex—whether it's his turn or yours.

❤ Start smoking. Choke when you do it, but claim that you love it.

❤ (This also works with oral sex.)

❤ Drink heavily at parties. Barf when you do it, but claim that you had a great time.

❤ (This also works with oral sex.)

❤ Tell him you had a threesome with your ex, but you would be too embarrassed to do it again.

❤ Rent an X-rated movie and fall asleep during the first bonk.

❤ Recognize the male lead—the one with the big "you know what"—in the X-rated movie as an old boyfriend.

❤ Talk about what a great X-rated movie it was the next morning and that you should watch them more often.

❤ Say "Are you kidding?" if he wakes you up for sex.

❤ Describe a "dream lover" who looks like his exact opposite.

❤ Giggle when he undresses. When he asks what you're laughing at, say "Nothing."

❤ Pretend you're not interested in sex.

❤ Pretend you're not interested in sex,
but talk about it wildly in front of him . . .
then go spend an hour in the shower.

❤ Take the batteries out of the remote control
and put them in your vibrator.

❤ Read erotic novels, but don't let them affect
your libido.

❤ Read erotic novels and laugh out loud at
the male's feeble attempts to seduce.

❤ Jump in the shower with him and
just bathe.

💔 Take a shower after sex and lock the bathroom door.

💔 Send a sensual anonymous e-mail from another screen name and see how he responds.

Pillow Talk

Honey I want to talk . . .

It's 4 in the morning! Can't it wait?

Fine. I'll just cry myself back to sleep then.

❤ Sleep with a stuffed animal.

❤ Force him to make room for the stuffed animal.

❤ Snore loudly.

❤ Wear flannel jammies and big, thick socks to bed every night.

❤ If he's staying up late, go to bed.

❤ If he needs his sleep, stay up.

❤ If he wants to sleep, stay up and read (and vice versa, of course).

❣ Start a conversation when he really needs his rest. When he tells you he's too tired to talk, cry silently into your pillow. Pretend you think he can't hear you.

❣ Turn all the lights on when he's sleeping. When he wakes up, say "I didn't realize you were sleeping."

❣ Get angry every time his leg crosses the imaginary line down the middle of the bed.

❣ Take all the covers and roll yourself up in them like a manicotti.

❣ Get one of those body pillows and call it your boyfriend.

♥ Call the dog up on the bed and make sure he sleeps right between you.

♥ Let your mom buy your lingerie.

Aggravating the One You Love

> Hey honey would you and some of your friends like to join the girls and I tonight for poker?

> Sure!

> Great tonight's theme is LUAU! We're all wearing hawaiian, and we're serving poi, and well we got these little cards that are in the shape of palm trees, and we'll be playing Don Juan . . .

❤ Try to change his behavior and tell him it's for his own good.

❤ When he says he's starving, say "me too" and then sit around and wait.

❤ Act like you know more about him—than about anything.

❤ In a difficult situation, look at him, roll your eyes, and make a big puffing sound with your mouth.

❤ Tell him "I'll take care of it"—then don't.

♥ Tell him "I thought you were going to take care of that" whenever you forget to do something.

♥ Tell him you need to have a "big talk" and schedule it days in advance.

♥ When you have the talk, say you can tell something is wrong.

♥ Act totally unruffled when he's standing there screaming in your face.

♥ Read the supermarket tabloids.

❣ Read the supermarket tabloids, and begin a conversation with "You're never going to believe this."

❣ If he's caught without an umbrella, offer him the flowered one and keep the black one for yourself.

❣ Act like his mother.

❣ Constantly "fix" him: his tie, his belt, his coat . . .

❣ Spit-wipe his hair if you have to.

❣ Buy him a six-pack of beer and don't tell him about it until you've had five.

❤ Hide his favorite foods behind other stuff in the fridge.

❤ Tell him stories that have no plot, and then get mad when he tells you to get to the point.

❤ Tell him he's cute when he's angry.

❤ Give him lots of unwanted advice about how he should do things.

❤ Every time he's not smiling, ask what's wrong.

❤ Every time he *is* smiling, ask what's up.

♥ Feel sorry for him—and tell him so.

♥ Tell him you found a phone number in his jeans pocket—just to see what he fesses up to.

♥ Tell him you think he's needy.

♥ Ask him if he REALLY loves you.

♥ Discuss pop psychology topics with great importance.

♥ When he makes a mistake, tell him "I told you so."

♥ When he gets angry with you, tell him he needs to look inside himself for the source of that anger.

♥ Let the dog lick your face right in front of him, and then go over to him for a big, slobbery kiss.

♥ Call him by the dog's name.

♥ Have a party for him and drink too much so that he has to take care of you all night.

The Agony of Defeat . . .

Honey, watch the game upstairs. I want to see the Sunday Night Movie on the big T.V.

But it's the Super Bowl and all the guys are coming over!

♥ Play better baseball than he does.

♥ Know more about football than he does.

♥ Don't know more about football, but talk like you do—preferably in front of his friends.

♥ Ask him what the difference is between the AFC and the NFC, and then walk out of the room while he is explaining.

♥ When watching a game with him, comment on which players are the cutest.

♥ Make it a competition.

♥ When he's watching an important game,

 At home: talk as loudly on the phone as you can.

Out: invite your friends out with you and talk as loudly as you can.

♥ Either way, ask questions about every single thing that happens in the game.

♥ Ask to go with him and his friends to the sports bar to watch the game . . . then get really bored and ask him to take you home.

♥ Pick up "his" hobby—and pick it up more quickly.

♥ Borrow his autographed baseball from the 1991 World Series and use it to play catch with your dog.

♥ Insist on going fishing with him and make him bait your hook every time. Catch a bigger fish than him, all the while fussing that you've never caught a fish in your life. Make him take the fish off the line, and refuse to have anything to do with cleaning it.

♥ Have better golf clubs than him . . . but never use them. Ask if he wants to borrow them.

♥ Coach him on his golf swing . . . after insisting on going with him and his friends and promising that you will remain quiet.

♥ Beat him on the golf course.

♥ Beat him on the golf course, and then announce it to everyone at the 19th-hole bar with a bottle of champagne.

♥ Invite your parents over for a Sunday afternoon when the game is on.

♥ Ask how many RBIs Troy Aikman has now.

♥ Call his team by the wrong name, like the "Dallas Oilers" or the "Buffalo Patriots."

♥ Get season football tickets—for the wrong team.

♥ Tell him he only watches sports, and when he turns the TV off, go online.

♥ Join a co-ed gym and wear skimpy workout clothes when you go.

♥ Rave about the gorgeous aerobics instructor and go to class looking like a million bucks.

The Idiot Box and the Movies

HONEY, COME QUICK

WHAT ?!?

I think they're gonna kiss—come sit down with me and watch.

❤ Make him watch romantic comedies.

❤ Fall asleep during the movies that he chooses.

❤ Tape *Oprah* and insist on watching it together. When he wants to watch the network premiere of the new *Star Wars* movie instead, accuse him of being passive-aggressive.

❤ Accidentally tape over a show that he really wanted to watch but hadn't seen yet. Then tell him that if it were so important, he would have stayed home to watch it.

❤ Take over the remote control and change channels really slowly.

♥ Take over the remote control and don't change channels at all.

♥ Call him into the room to see the *Beverly Hills 90210* previews.

♥ Tape soap operas and watch them during prime time.

♥ Explain to him what's going on in the soaps.

♥ Talk about the soap opera characters like you actually know them, like they are your friends. Then bring them up again the next morning.

♥ Invite friends over for a big *ER* party and swoon over George Clooney like teenagers.

♥ Go to a movie with one of his friends.

♥ Go to a movie with one of his friends— then come home and don't tell him anything.

♥ Go to a movie that he really wants to see— with a friend

or

♥ Go to a movie he really wants to see, and then talk to him during the whole thing.

Life in the Aggravation Lane

❤ Don't let him fix your car.

❤ Talk about how you can tune up your own car.

❤ Refer to his car by the wrong name.

❤ Buy a faster car than his.

❤ Talk him into trading his sport utility vehicle for a minivan.

❤ Tell him you need to trade cars because yours is out of gas.

❤ Be a backseat driver.

❥ When he's driving, white-knuckle the dashboard.

❥ When he gets lost driving, make a big deal of it.

❥ Every time he passes a car, suck in your breath.

❥ When he's driving, use his car phone to call all your friends.

❥ Insist on driving, especially when you don't know where you're going.

❥ When you drive, continuously ask him for directions but NEVER give up the wheel.

♥ Ask for directions in heavy traffic.

♥ When you're driving, ask for a kiss every
   time the light turns green.

♥ Act like you know how to parallel
   park when you don't, and don't let him
   take over.

♥ Put on makeup in the car during rush hour.

♥ Drive really slow.

♥ Drive way too fast.

♥ Blame everyone else on the road for bad driving.

♥ Don't ever change lanes.

♥ Leave your blinker on.

♥ Change all radio presets on his car to the stations that play the mushy love songs. When he confronts you about it, say, "You're welcome."

♥ Leave him notes with little "inspirational messages" on his dashboard.

Brother, Can You Spare a Fifty?

❤ Borrow his last twenty from him while he's sleeping and "forget" to tell him.

❤ Ask him for $100 to get you through till next payday, and then go out and buy a new outfit. "Forget" to pay it back. If he brings it up, tell him you bought groceries.

❤ Offer to spring for the wine, and buy the cheapest bottle you can find.

❤ Offer to buy the beer, and bring home a generic lite.

❤ Borrow his cash card and "forget" to put it back in his wallet.

❣ Tell him that if he earned more money, you could get a maid.

❣ Hate your job and tell him that if he made more, you wouldn't have to go through all this.

❣ Be financially independent of him.

❣ Be financially dependent on him and act like the queen.

❣ Make more money than him.

❣ Make less money than him, but work more hours and expect him to do half the household chores.

❤ Don't bother making any money at all, but still expect him to do the household chores.

❤ Order cute little bunny checks for your joint checking account.

❤ Pretend you don't know how to balance the checkbook while you calculate to the exact penny every cent you saved at the last sale you went to. (This works with taxes too.)

❤ Complain repeatedly when you can't get a credit card, but get pissed off if he gets one for you. Max it out as a punishment.

❤ Make a major purchase without telling him.

💔 Make a major purchase after you've talked to him about it and he said no.

💔 Get season opera tickets for you both, pay a lot of money for them, and charge them on his credit card.

Annoying Office Etiquette

❤ Send a balloon bouquet to him at the office.

❤ Drink the last cup of coffee and don't make a new pot.

❤ Call your male co-workers by cute nicknames.

❤ Call him at work and make him tell you that he loves you in front of his coworkers.

❤ Apply for a job where he works.

❤ Get a job where he works, and make friends with all his friends.

❣ Gossip at the water cooler.

❣ Tell his boss an off-color joke.

❣ Sign your male boss's name for him and dot the "i" with a little smiley face.

❣ Cry in a meeting just to get your way.

❣ Become a CEO in a male-dominated company.

❣ Become a CEO and hire a male assistant.

❣ Invite him home for a "nooner" and forget to show up.

💔 Apply large amounts of perfume before getting into the elevator.

💔 "Pump" (breast milk) at the office and keep the milk right there on the top shelf, front and center, of the fridge.

💔 Send him another balloon bouquet after you promised NEVER, NEVER to do that again.

💔 Talk about the soaps you regularly tape with the guys at the water cooler.

💔 Suggest happy hour drinks, and then take them to a fern bar where every drink is served in bright colors with little umbrellas and cute names.

15

Home Is Where the Aggravating Woman Is

❤ Drink them under the table, slap 'em on the butt, and send 'em home in a cab.

❤ Stand in front of the television when you talk to him.

❤ Read his horoscope to him every day like it's an absolute universal truth to live by. Be sure to point out the times it's right on. When it's way off, make sure you're indignant.

❤ Cancel the paper delivery.

❤ Read the paper before he gets to it, and make sure you put it back all out of order.

❥ Don't know how to cook.

❥ If you do know how to cook, just don't do it.

❥ Come home from work and ask him what's for dinner. Give him five seconds to answer, and then tell him you guess you'll have to order in again. Then wait for him to make the call.

❥ While he's brushing his teeth in the morning, walk in the bathroom and say: "Uh oh!" When he asks you "What?" say nothing. If he pursues it, cry and tell him you accidentally dropped his toothbrush in the toilet last night. When he gets mad, make like it's his own fault.

💔 Use his brand-new razor to shave your legs. Leave it full of soap and residue, and then deny that you used it.

💔 Buy him replacement razors, but make sure they're pink.

💔 Open the door when he's sitting on the throne reading the paper, and ask him what's taking him so long.

💔 Open the door when he's sitting on the throne, and start talking about your day.

💔 Don't flush the toilet every time in an effort "to conserve water."

❥ Use up all the toilet paper and don't change the roll.

❥ Tell him that you don't mind that he leaves the bathroom seat up, and then complain when you fall into the toilet in the middle of the night. (Make sure you wake him up to tell him.)

❥ When he asks how your day was, just say "fine" and then call all your girlfriends with ecstatic news.

❥ Use his favorite coffee mug for anything but coffee.

❥ Bring home a kitten. Tell him you'll feed it and all he has to do is change the litter box.

♥ Ask him what he's doing when it's very obvious what he's doing, like reading the paper—anything to break his concentration and make him notice you.

♥ Ask questions about his day, and then watch TV while he responds.

♥ Don't bother looking for anything: always ask him where it is first. Make sure you call from the other room when asking.

♥ Lie on the paper like a cat.

♥ Upset his morning rituals.

♥ When he comes home from work with problems, tell him that you're there with a support network of friends.

♥ When you want to talk to him, call him from the other room and wait for him to come to you. Make a big deal if he doesn't respond.

Martha Stewart
Meets Bob Vila

❥ Paint something in the house pink.

❥ Buy a flowered bedspread.

❥ When redecorating, be sure to remember the chintz.

❥ Don't know what a Phillips screwdriver is.

❥ Then ask him who Phillip is.

❥ When he tells you "That's just what it's called," ask why.

♥ Ask him to help you rearrange all the living room furniture, including the piano. When he's done, sort of scrunch up your face then ask him to "help" you move it back.

♥ Insist that the house needs to be repainted but that you can't afford to hire anyone.

♥ Take him with you to choose the color.

♥ Leave the paint in the living room until he "gets it."

♥ When he's done painting, change your mind about the color.

❤ When he's trying to fix something, make sure you "get your face right in there" and offer instructions.

❤ Fix things around the house.

❤ When he fixes things around the house, go back and just "tweak" them a bit.

❤ "Organize" his tools.

❤ Use his tools . . . incorrectly.

Aggravating Your Husband

Q. How many husbands does it take to change a lightbulb?

A. Where's the remote control?

♥ Insist that he marry you before you have sex.

♥ Make a big deal out of engagement rings.

♥ When you get one, don't wear it—save it for "special occasions."

♥ After the wedding, make a big deal out of showing your new china pattern.

♥ Don't wear a wedding band, and don't explain why.

♥ Ask him suspiciously why he doesn't wear his wedding band . . .

♥ Don't tell him he forgot your anniversary until the next day. (Besides being aggravating, it can also get you an unusually large gift.)

♥ Forget your anniversary, and when he reminds you, tell him you were just testing him.

♥ Call him "hubby" in public.

♥ Suggest that your mom move in.

♥ Now that you are equal partners, split up the household chores and keep a list of them on the fridge for all to see.

💔 Sit on his lap and smother him with kisses every time his friends come over.

💔 Sneak off to the couch in the middle of the night.

💔 Start a collection.

💔 Start "crafting."

💔 Bring home every stray you can get your hands on.

💔 Make your work life more important than your home life.

❤ Create an open door policy at your home for all of your friends when they have personal problems.

❤ Quit looking out for your figure.

❤ Get a new wardrobe of "comfy" clothes.

❤ Paint the living room in his favorite T-shirt.

❤ Tell him you just want to be "a housewife."

❤ Ask him if it isn't about time for his midlife crisis.

❤ Tell him you are learning to see his feminine side.

❤ Ask him to go to therapy.

❤ When *he* suggests it's time for therapy, tell him no.

❤ Opt for "spiritual counseling." (Tell him you learned it on *Oprah*.)

Aggravating with the Kids

I'm so proud of Tommy for signing up for ballet lessons

He can't take ballet lessons, he'll be the only boy!

That's why I told him that you would take him!

❤ If you're going to have a child, make sure it's a girl.

❤ While you are pregnant, make him wear one of those "sympathy bellies."

❤ Prepare for childbirth by making long lists of all the names you're going to call him during labor.

❤ When you fill out the birth certificate, give the kid your last name. Forget to mention it.

❤ Talk about the birth of your children in very graphic terms in front of his friends.

♥ Whenever he is sick, bring up childbirth.

♥ Raise your daughter to be just like you.

♥ Raise a generation that doesn't understand the connotations behind "cat fight," "runs like a girl," or "sissy."

♥ Sign your son up for dance lessons.

♥ Tell him you don't want to discipline the kids because you don't want to break their spirit.

♥ After the separation, don't remind him of school obligations knowing he'll never remember them.

❤ Leave the kids dirty when it's time to go to his mother's.

❤ Send the kids to him with their dirty laundry.

❤ Drop the kids off at dinnertime—when they are really hungry.

❤ Bring the kids to him dirty.

❤ Take the kids to visit your family in another state for the holidays.

19

Blood Is Thicker
Than Water

Honey, I want you to meet my NEW best friend!

That's my MOTHER.

I know, isn't it GREAT?

❤ When you meet his parents for the first time, bring your Ouija™ board.

❤ Over dinner with his folks, share a wild dream you had about your ex-boyfriend.

❤ Make him go back home with you and meet every person you've ever known in your life.

❤ If it's your turn to go home for the holidays with him, be better liked than him.

or

❤ make yourself scarce and bring work.

❣ Insist that he not meet your mom, but don't tell him why.

❣ Insist that he meet your mom, tell him every reason you can think of why he should, and bug him about it for weeks.

❣ Win his mother over.

❣ Call his mother every time you want him to do something and he won't listen. (Soon, all you'll have to do is just pick up the phone . . .)

❣ Give his mom a copy of this book, and read it together and laugh.

❤ Talk about his mother when he's feeling romantic.

❤ When he complains that you don't cook like his mother, invite her over to cook dinner. After she's gone, complain about her for hours . . . then throw up.

❤ Invite the sister of yours that he hates to come spend a week with you—after her big break-up, when she's particularly hating men. Give him dirty looks the whole time, and sleep on the couch.

Breaking Up Is Never Hard
for the Aggravating Woman

Dear Jon Doe,
  I don't want to date
you anymore. But can
we still be friends?

            love,
            Sally

P.S. Will you still come
over and help me move?

❤ *Stop* being a drama queen—over him.

❤ Refer quite often to the past as "when you used to love me."

❤ Send him copies of his love letters, "accidentally" including one from another ex.

❤ When he tells *you* that you think everything is *his* fault, agree and then tell him you forgive him.

❤ Go away for a romantic weekend to try to get your relationship back on track—and bring work with you.

❥ Tell him that he's being emotional.

❥ Never give him any time to himself. Then tell him you feel like you're growing apart. . . and then say, "We just don't spend any quality time together."

❥ Tell him that you just "need some time."

❥ Tell him that you need some time apart. When he agrees, cry that you knew he never cared for you anyway.

❥ Tell him that you need more sex in your life—not romance, just sex—and that you wish you could have told him that years ago, but you didn't want to hurt his feelings.

❤ Call him every day for a week, begging for him to come back to you. When he finally calls, tell him you "need some space."

❤ Provide an infinite supply of guilt.

❤ Cut him out of all the photos of the two of you, and then send him his half.

❤ Buy him a book on how to get in touch with his feelings.

❤ Give him lots of tips on how to improve himself, for "the next one." Suggest dressing techniques and grooming.

❤ Fight for custody of his dog.

❤ Bribe his faithful dog away on a steady diet of Ring Dings.

❤ Hide stuff of his that you really want to keep for yourself (favorite books, CDs, clothing, etc.).

❤ Take his favorite autographed baseball from the 1991 World Series and swear he gave it to you in a fit of passion.

❤ Pawn the nicest piece of jewelry he ever gave you . . . and replace it with what you really wanted in the first place. Then make sure he sees you wearing it.

❣ Remind him that the things he finds annoying about you today, he used to think were charming.

❣ Remind him of all the things he never did for you.

❣ While you're at it, remind him of the times when he really screwed up.

❣ Remind him that his child support payment is late—in front of his friends.

❣ Tell anyone who calls for him that he's dead.

♥ Tell him that since the separation, you've finally been able to find your Zen.

♥ When he stops by to pick up some of his things, make sure he sees the new pack of condoms by the bed.

♥ Take up an extreme sport.

♥ Become a lesbian.

♥ Mention that in some states PMS is a valid defense for murder.

♥ If he fights you for custody, give in.

❣ Set fire to his car.

❣ Don't tell him about the audit until the day before.

❣ Tell him you were just kidding about liking men with a little meat on their bones.

❣ Have a male dancer sent to his office on his birthday.

❣ Accuse him of doing all of the bad things that you do.

❣ Stay best friends with his mother.

❣ Be perfectly okay all by yourself.

❣ Lose weight, get a make-over, and look fabulous.

❣ Take the kids to see a therapist because of the divorce.

❣ Quote the therapist whenever it's convenient.

21

Aggravating the EX!

Up next on the Oprah Winfrey show . . . best-selling author of <u>How To Aggravate a Man</u> tells the honest truth about her greatest inspiration, her EX-HUSBAND!

♥ When he complains that you don't cook like his ex, invite her over to cook. Complain about her for the rest of the evening . . . then throw up.

♥ Make friends with his ex-girlfriends.

♥ Run into an old boyfriend together—and kiss him on the lips.

♥ After you've broken up, make sure he knows every time you have a date.

♥ Date one of his old friends.

♥ Date a guy who is better looking than him.

💔 Go back to your old boyfriend.

💔 Become good friends with his new girlfriend.

💔 Talk to his new girlfriend about "when you were with him."

Aggravating the Average
Joe off the Street

NO! I said I wanted
that one . . . the one
on the TOP shelf!

But this one is
EXACTLY the
same ma'am.

♥ Ask a guy for complicated directions, and then make him tell you again.

♥ Read the paper over men's shoulders.

♥ When a male telemarketer calls, ask tons of unrelated questions. Then thank him and hang up without buying anything.

♥ Go into a co-ed chat room on the Internet and make grand generalizations about men.

♥ Make multiple transactions at the busy cash machine while singing a Carpenters song.

♥ Go to the latest guys' action flick and talk to your girlfriend all the way through it.

♥ Order a rare and complicated drink that the male bartender needs the mixology book for. Then send it back, saying it's "just a little off," and order a beer instead.

♥ When asked to dance in a nightclub, say you don't feel like it—then dance with your girlfriends instead.

♥ Flirt with the guy across the bar—until he comes over to talk.

♥ Bum a cigarette from the well-dressed man at the bar, and then just continue to smoke off his pack while telling him how much money you are saving by not smoking.

♥ Serve yourself at the full-service pump.

♥ Ask the full-service attendant to fill your tank while you're at the self-service pump.

♥ Take a class on auto repair, and then dominate the conversation with talk about "girl" things.

♥ Tell the mechanic at the service station that the "thingamajig" sounds a little "goofy."

♥ Keep the stereo blasting while he's trying to hear the goofy thingamajig.

♥ Ask a mechanic to go with you to buy a car. Listen to all of his suggestions—then get the red one.

♥ Look at his fly.

❣ Look at the car salesman with great suspicion, and kick all the tires.

❣ When buying cucumbers, remark to the gentleman next to you that "size does count."

❣ Stop up the checkout line at the grocery store by talking to the cashier about her manicure . . . and hairstyle . . . and men!

❣ Ask the man in front of you in line if you can go before him, even though you have several items and he has only one.

❣ Stop up the supermarket line by reading the tabloids.

♥ Discuss the tabloids with the clerk.

♥ At the gym, compliment the guy with the big muscles and tell him how great the steroids are working.

♥ At a sports bar, pick a favorite team based on the colors and style of the uniform, and then root for them loudly and enthusiastically

or

♥ Constantly change your "favorite team" according to who is winning at the time.

♥ Find a male therapist and hold him personally responsible for all the pain men have inflicted in your life.

23

If All Else Fails, Scream "Feminist" in a Crowded Theater

Things to do today:

1. Accept the job as CEO
2. Paint my nails
3. Ask Jim out on a date
4. Call my mother
5. Invest $200,000

❣ Now that you've taken over the house, take over the Senate.

❣ Plaster a picture of Gloria Steinam on the bedroom wall.

❣ Keep your maiden name.

❣ Expect the double standard—fight to be an equal, and then get mad when he doesn't hold the door open for you.

❣ When a man opens a door for you, remark, "Haven't you ever heard of women's lib?"

💔 Later in the day, balance yourself out by using "Ladies first."

💔 When a man offers you his seat, put your coat and purse on it and stand.

💔 Assert yourself in any male-dominated situation.

💔 In a discussion, join sides based on gender.

Talking Book

Oh look honey, my book is on the bestseller list! And by the way will you be a dear and grab my slippers? And maybe a cold drink, oh and what's for dinner?

♥ Keep a copy of this book at arm's reach at all times.

♥ Talk about it to girlfriends when you are out.

♥ Give a copy of it to his mother.

♥ Talk about the authors like they're geniuses.

♥ Initiate a campaign of letters to *Oprah*.

♥ Write a book on how to aggravate men, become famous, makes loads of money, and then turn your husband into your housewife. (Honey, can you get my slippers?)

❤️ Write a book on how to aggravate men, start a worldwide movement of "male aggravation," and make sure all of the men in the universe know you are his <u>EX</u>-wife.

❤️ Get a T-shirt that says "DON'T MESS WITH ME, I READ THE BOOK!"